I0605689

MARIE'S MAGIC EGGS

HOW MARIE PROCAI KEPT THE UKRAINIAN ART OF PYSANKY ALIVE

SANDRA NEIL WALLACE ILLUSTRATED BY EVAN TURK

CALKINS CREEK
AN IMPRINT OF ASTRA BOOKS FOR YOUNG READERS
New York

Each spring in a Ukrainian village, a feisty young girl with long, braided hair celebrated her favorite tradition. As the sun warmed the lush land for planting, Marie and her grandmother made pysanky—beautiful, decorated eggs—in the same way Ukrainians had done since ancient times.

To Marie, making pysanky at Easter with Baba was magical. For the legend goes that as long as pysanky are decorated, there will be good in the world.

While pots filled with sunflowers and juicy red beets bubbled on Baba's stove to color the eggs in dazzling dyes, Marie cradled a chicken egg.

She grasped a kistka the way Baba had taught her and, with its warm beeswax flowing like ink, Marie sketched a story, a wish, a prayer, a gift.

Symbols of swirling, golden wheat.
Blue flowers for beauty.
Rays of sunshine, streaming bright.
Roosters clucking at the sky.

After each design, Marie dipped the egg in different colors. Ruby red and brilliant black were her favorites. Then, just like Baba, Marie stitched a cloth with embroidery to wrap the eggs.

It seemed like Marie would always be with Baba and make beautiful pysanky. But several springs later, when fighting and famine made their village unsafe, Marie and her family fled.

With no home or harvest, Marie searched sunflower fields for food to eat, not to boil for pysanky colors.

When her brothers left for better lives in North America, Marie soon followed. The rest of her family stayed behind—including Baba.

In 1911, thirteen-year-old Marie boarded a ship alone, bound for New York. She held a small suitcase and big memories of the grandmother she already missed.

First, Marie lived in Pennsylvania, where her brother Paul worked in the coal mines. But she found him too bossy, and Marie would have none of that. She took in washing, scrubbing coal from the miners' clothes until she'd earned enough money to buy a train ticket.

Then she left for Canada to live with her brother Kirylo.

On the train
rolling across the prairie,
everything Marie saw reminded
her of Ukraine: deer darting through
wheat fields. Barn swallows soaring above
the tracks, reaching for the sun that Marie
loved to sketch on pysanky.

When the train stopped in Minneapolis for the night, Marie hopped off. With the few English words that she knew, Marie asked a police officer if any Ukrainians lived there. He pointed to a house by the river lit up by the moonlight.

Marie knocked on the door. Inside, lived her favorite cousin from Ukraine! For Marie, this seemed like magic, too, so she stayed in Minneapolis.

Marie worked as a waitress in a busy restaurant. She hired a tutor to teach her English.

But by the river where Marie lived with her cousin, the streets swelled with Ukrainian sounds.

The savory scent of Ukrainian foods floated through Marie's boardinghouse as her neighbors cooked.

Mechanics and mill workers.

Builders and bakers.

All born in Ukraine like Marie.

In the spring, Marie yearned to make pysanky just like Baba had taught her. But there were no pysanka artists in Minneapolis, and Marie couldn't find a kistka. She didn't have a big stove like Baba's to boil pysanky colors.

How would Marie make pysanky?

With the money she'd saved, Marie purchased colorful pieces of paper. She crumpled and stuffed them in pickle jars with water to make dyes. As pysanky patterns swirled in her head, Marie pulled a shoelace from her boot. Grasping its metal tip, she dipped it in beeswax warmed by a candle.

Holding a hen's fresh egg, Marie sketched a story, a wish, a prayer, a gift.

Birds for protection and wishes to come true.

Golden wheat for enough food to eat.

Rays of the sun to shine on her new life in America.

Cradling the pysanka in her hands felt like holding a piece of her homeland and giving Baba a hug.

Marie missed her homeland. Ukraine was in danger. After the First World War, when Marie was twenty-one, Russia's Red Army invaded Ukraine. Anyone caught speaking Ukrainian could be hauled into jail. Making pysanky was dangerous. Like a wicked kind of magic, the beautiful eggs disappeared from Ukrainian museums. Books about pysanky burned, and soldiers crushed cherished collections. It was as if the ancient folk art never existed.

In Minneapolis, to keep the art of pysanky alive, Marie sketched the ancient symbols on egg after egg. Stirring different homemade dyes into glass jars, Marie's favorite colors took on a new intensity. Red became richer. Black became bolder. The symbols were just like Baba's, but these new hues became Marie's own colors, created in her new country.

The cherished tradition Marie brought from Ukraine took root in America.

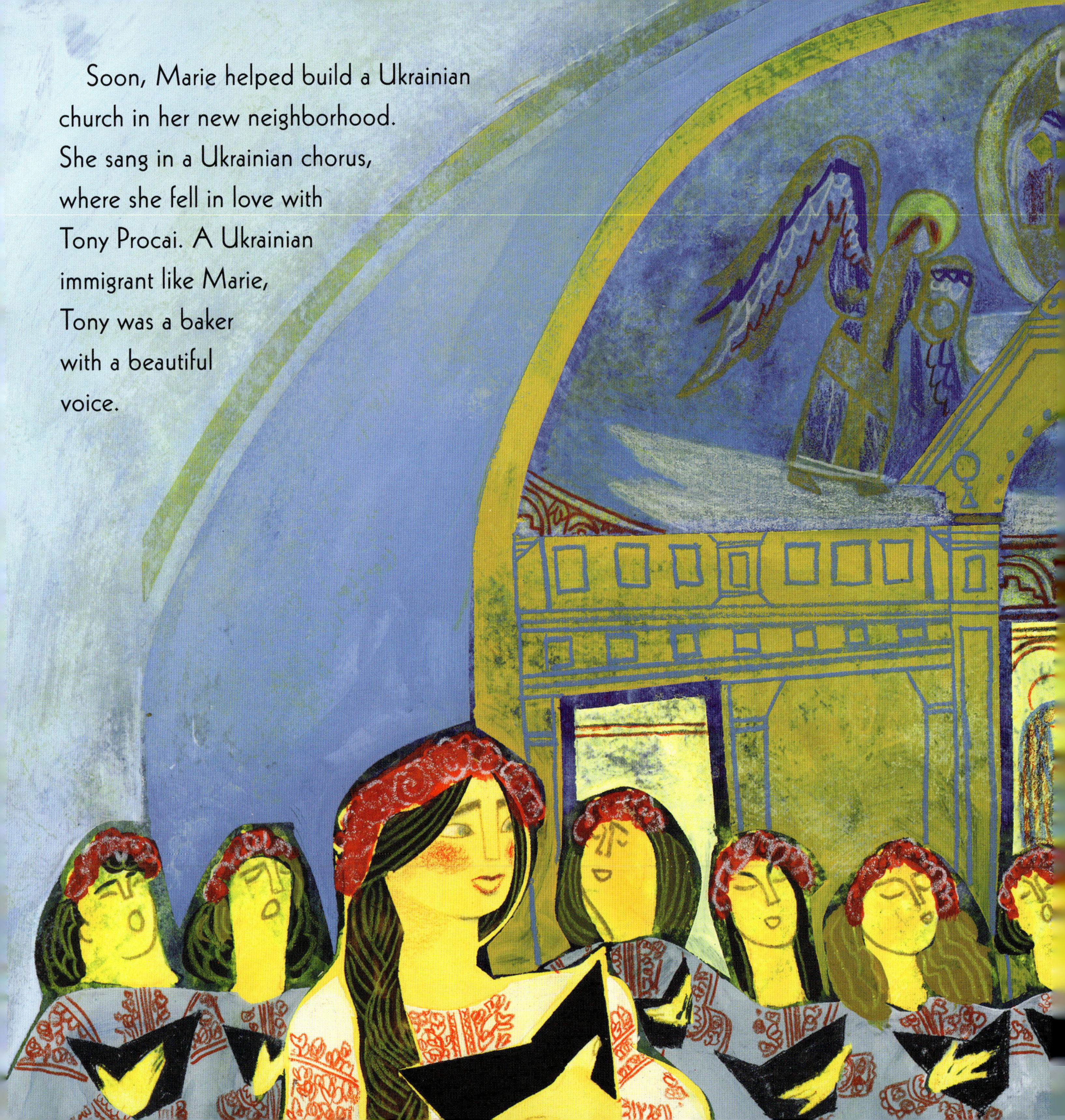

Soon, Marie helped build a Ukrainian church in her new neighborhood. She sang in a Ukrainian chorus, where she fell in love with Tony Procai. A Ukrainian immigrant like Marie, Tony was a baker with a beautiful voice.

When Marie and Tony married and had a family, Tony saw how much Marie loved to make pysanky. He could make things, too—and not just steaming loaves of Easter Paska bread at the bakery where he worked.

Tony made Marie a kistka by crafting copper into a cone. Then he pushed the cone through a wooden peg and wrapped them together with wire.

Using Tony's kistka, Marie's designs grew more intricate—like rows of sunflowers sprouting in Ukraine. She taught their children how to make pysanky.

But in 1945, Marie's new country was also at war. Her son, Earl, joined the US Navy. The nineteen-year-old became a bugler on a warship bound for Japan. Marie wanted to help. At night, she stitched blankets to keep the sailors warm. Then one day, Marie received news that Earl had died when a bomb tore through the ship.

It was just before Easter.

How would Marie make pysanky?

As a candle burned and warmed the golden beeswax, Marie let her sadness pour through her kistka and onto the pysanka. Working all night with her daughters, Marie covered the eggs with symbols that had given Ukrainians strength since ancient times.

Ласкаво просимо
Welcome!

When the war finally ended, Marie learned about Ukrainian refugees hoping to start a new life in America. With no freedom in their country and their homes destroyed, they sailed to New York, just like Marie had done years earlier. Now they needed a place to stay.

In Minneapolis, Marie welcomed them into her home.

Farmers and fine artists.

Students and seamstresses.

At Marie and Tony's house, the newcomers squeezed onto sofas and crammed into the kitchen.

Everyone was free to

plant and paint,

sing and sew,

speak Ukrainian, and . . . make pysanky!

Marie saw how her daughter Luba loved making pysanky just like she did. With no place in Minneapolis to purchase Ukrainian arts and crafts, they opened a Ukrainian gift shop in Marie's busy living room.

On the first day, business was slow. Marie only sold two handkerchiefs she'd stitched with designs from her village in Ukraine.

But in the spring when people spotted pysanky for sale, they marveled at their beauty and bought all the eggs. Curious, they wanted to learn how to make them.

Determined to teach people, Marie and Luba customized kistky. They crafted clumps of beeswax into tiny blocks and perfected colorful dyes and Ukrainian designs. Then they put them in a box with instructions and invented the first pysanky kits.

aster Egg Decorating Kit
UKRAINIAN GIFT SHOP
UKRAINIAN GIFT SHOP
UKRAINIAN GIFT SHOP
UKRAINIAN GIFT SHOP
UKRAINIAN GIFT SHOP

Ukrainian
GIFT SHOP
OPEN

The business quickly outgrew Marie's living room, so she rented a storefront. Her daughter Johanna joined the business.

Remembering how her refugee housemates loved to stitch and sew, Marie hired some of them to embroider vyshyvankas—Ukrainian shirts and blouses—to sell at the store.

For decades, Marie and her daughters crafted pysanky so original that folk art critics declared them the finest pysanka artists in America. At the White House, presidents displayed the family's Ukrainian eggs for visitors to admire.

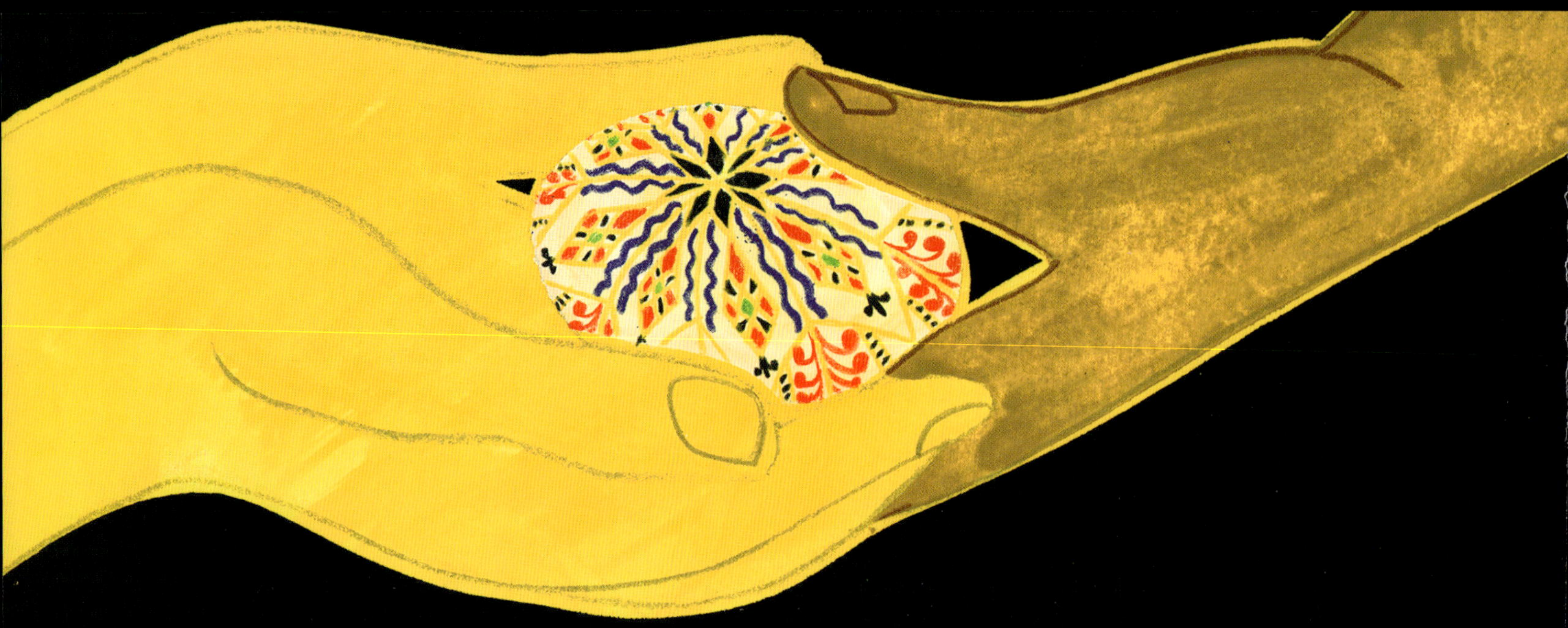

By 1991, the Ukrainian Gift Shop had become the biggest supplier of pysanky kits in the world.

That year there was much to celebrate in Marie's homeland. Ukraine had gained its freedom from the Soviet Union.

But after seventy years, generations of Ukrainians had forgotten how to make pysanky. They were hungry to learn.

In Minneapolis, Marie's family wrote books and crafted pysanky to remind them how.

Customers ordered so many of Marie's Ukrainian eggs that she didn't just make them each spring. Every day, like a perfect kind of magic—steeped in the sweet-honey scent of beeswax—Marie created pysanky as beautiful as her baba's.

On tiny pullet eggs barely bigger than a honeybee.
On rhea eggs the size of plump, red beets.
On ostrich eggs as high as Easter Paska bread.

Marie sketched a story, a wish, a prayer, a gift.

Birds for protection and wishes that came true.
Wheat for enough food to eat.
Rays of the sun that had shone bright on her life in America.

For the legend goes that as long as pysanky are decorated,
there will be good in the world.

Author's Note

The vyshyvanka I'm wearing has been in my family for more than half a century.

Growing up, my Ukrainian grandmother, Baba Neilipovitz, shared many cultural traditions with us that she'd brought with her from Ukraine as a teenager, just like Marie—including making pysanky. I would later discover that the kistka that she'd held was a writing tool from the Ukrainian Gift Shop.

But I didn't learn about Marie Sokol Procai until Russia invaded Ukraine in February of 2022. As Russia's war on the country of my ancestors continued into Easter, I found hope in people gathering around the world to learn how to make pysanky in solidarity with Ukraine. Many of their tool kits also came from the Ukrainian Gift Shop.

The shop has never closed. During Russia's attempts to erase Ukrainian identity by bombing cultural sites and artifacts, Marie's grandchildren and great-grandchildren continued to share the love of pysanky with people around the world using the same techniques that Marie taught their parents and grandparents.

Marie demonstrates the art of pysanky at a Minneapolis library in 1941 as children watch, mesmerized.

It's a testament to Marie's life story of resilience and ingenuity that began when she was a child, determined to freely express her Ukrainian culture: making pysanky like her baba taught her, speaking Ukrainian, and going to church.

Born in the western Ukrainian village of Dobrosyn in 1897, Marie and her Ukrainian Orthodox Christian ancestors lived hard lives under occupying rulers from various countries. Marie and her family fled to present-day Croatia. After Marie's older brothers immigrated to North America, Marie soon made the same voyage by herself on the SS *Bremen*. Likely worried that she'd be turned away because of her young age, thirteen-year-old Marie told immigration officers at Ellis Island that she was sixteen.

In Minneapolis, Marie built a new life steeped in Ukrainian traditions. She used improvised tools to make pysanky, but what was authentic were the ancient Ukrainian symbols that Marie styled on the eggs.

When Russia's Soviet regime attacked or suppressed Ukrainian culture, Marie made preserving and amplifying the art of pysanky her life's work. And she succeeded.

At a time when most work spaces were closed to women and their entrepreneurship was discouraged, Marie stood out. Marie and her family also became renowned for designing Ukrainian eggs. Pulitzer Prize-winning journalist Meyer Berger wrote that Marie and her daughters, Luba Perchyshyn and Johanna Luciow, were considered the greatest "egg jewelers" in the United States. Luba would become known as one of the greatest pysanka artists in the world. In 1972, when the family was featured in *National Geographic*, Marie was credited with pysanky's popularity. The art form became a global conversation.

In this 1947 photo, Marie's daughter, Luba Perchyshyn, displays her world-renowned pysanky as artists Marie Jaseniuk and Stephanie Galysh work on theirs.

"Marie's designs formed the foundation of all our pysanky," Ann Kmit, Marie's granddaughter, told me, including the popular books the family wrote on how to make them. Marie and her family advanced every aspect of the art form, elevating its creativity by sharing and developing designs, perfecting and manufacturing dyes and tools, and becoming the largest supplier of pysanka products in the world.

But what Marie loved most was making pysanky, which she did until she could no longer hold a kistka. Marie died in 1994, shortly after Easter, at the age of ninety-six.

Marie and World War II

When Marie's life intersected with World War II, the war revealed the tragic losses and sacrifices that immigrants and their families make for their new country and how these sacrifices shape history. Marie and Tony's son, Earl Procai, was killed on the USS *Indianapolis* in March of 1945.

Nineteen-year-old Earl Procai, US Navy Bugler Second Class

A few years after Earl's tragic death, Marie learned how Ukrainians could start new lives in the United States through the Displaced Persons Acts. But they needed to be sponsored.

"My grandparents sponsored many Ukrainians," Marie's granddaughter Natalie Perchyshyn remembered. Marie and Tony had always helped Ukrainians, but now they sponsored their voyages, and found them jobs and places to live. Through a Ukrainian American relief agency, Marie and her family helped more than one hundred Ukrainian people who'd fled persecution, had their homes destroyed, or been made to work in forced labor camps in Nazi Germany. Many stayed at Tony and Marie's home temporarily, including well-known Ukrainian artist Oksana Liaturynska.

Pronunciation Guide

Here is how to pronounce the Ukrainian words in this book, and how they are written in the Ukrainian Cyrillic alphabet:

PYSANKY (писанки)
pih-san-kih
Ukrainian Easter eggs

KISTKA (Кістка)
kisst-kah
stylus

PROCAI (Процай)
Pro-tsigh
Marie's last name

VYSHYVANKA (вишивáнка)
vee-shee-vahn-kah
embroidered shirt

The Art of Pysanky

Pysanky comes from the word, pysaty, which means "to write" in Ukrainian. Since ancient times, Ukrainians have written on eggs to celebrate the arrival of spring, believing that the sun and the moon—like the egg—held magical powers, awakening the earth after winter and bringing with it new life. Early Ukrainians worshipped the sun and offered pysanky as a gift. They buried the eggs in the ground for good harvests and healthy lives. When Christianity came to Ukraine in the tenth century AD, Ukrainian Christians used pysanky to celebrate Easter.

The Pysanka Legend

There is a centuries-old legend associated with pysanky and the fate of the world. The popular story has been shared universally and continues to be passed on. It's a story of an evil creature who can only be stopped from destroying the world by the number of pysanky people make each year. The more Ukrainian eggs, the more the world is at peace and good prevails. Though it's a myth, many people design Ukrainian eggs in the spirit of creating good in the world, one pysanka at a time.

A basket of pysanky crafted by Marie's family for the 1972 *National Geographic* article featuring them.

Pysanky instruction books by Marie's family continue to inspire generations of artists throughout the world.

Marie created pysanky and shared her knowledge of the art form for many decades.

Marie and Tony Procai perform in a Ukrainian play in 1916.

How to Make Pysanky

The colors and symbols created to design the eggs tell a story or illustrate a wish, much like Egyptian hieroglyphics. They are applied onto a raw egg using the batik wax-resistant method. Beeswax is scraped into the copper funnel of a writing tool called a kistka. Its tip is used to write the designs on the egg, which is then dipped in the first dye color. More designs are written, and the process is repeated until the story is complete. When the egg is polished after being warmed over a candle flame, the wax melts and like magic the pysanka's designs appear. Marie's favorite colors were red and black. She used many different hues, including green, as accent colors.

A Pysanka Playlist

While making pysanky, Marie listened to Ukrainian music, including bandura music and folk songs recorded by Ukrainian musicians like these:

Veryovka Ensemble Ukrainian Folk Choir
soundcloud.com/veryovkaensemble

Bandurist Victor Mishalow
youtube.com/watch?v=k2z1h41vwn0

Women's Bandura Ensemble of North America
womensbanduraensemble.bandcamp.com/releases

Ukrainian Dnipro Ensemble of Edmonton
facebook.com/dniprochoir/videos

Museums, Sites, and Festivals Featuring Pysanky

Pysanka artists are well respected as folk artists. Their art is featured in private collections, at the White House, and in museums around the world. But in Ukraine, the recognition is new. Just a few decades ago, before Ukraine's Pysanka Museum opened, curators hid folk art collections, fearing they would be crushed by the Soviet regime because of their religious significance and importance to Ukrainian cultural identity. During Russia's war on Ukraine, the museum was in danger again as thousands of Ukrainian cultural sites, churches, and libraries were damaged or destroyed by Russian artillery.

In 2024, The United Nations Educational, Scientific and Cultural Organization (UNESCO) declared the Ukrainian art of pysanky an Intangible Cultural Heritage of Humanity.

Pysanka Museum—Kolomyia, Ukraine
pysanka.museum

Ukrainian Institute of America—New York, New York
pysanka.ukrainianinstitute.org

Ukrainian National Museum of Chicago—Illinois
ukrainiannationalmuseum.org/project/pysanky

Vegreville Pysanka Festival—Alberta
pysankafestival.com

Pysanka Festival, Los Angeles—California
ukrainianartcentersocal.org

SELECTED BIBLIOGRAPHY

All sources for quotations used in the book are marked with an asterisk (*).

BOOKS

Applebaum, Anne. *Red Famine: Stalin's War on Ukraine.* New York: Anchor Books, 2017.

Kmit, Ann et al. *Ukrainian Easter Eggs and How We Make Them.* Minneapolis: Ukrainian Gift Shop, 1979.

Luciow, Johanna, et al. *Eggs Beautiful: How to Make Ukrainian Easter Eggs.* Minneapolis: Ukrainian Gift Shop, 1975.

Newall, Venetia. *An Egg at Easter: A Folklore Study.* Bloomington: Indiana University Press, 1971.

Perchyshyn, Natalie. *A Kid's Guide to Decorating Ukrainian Easter Eggs.* Minneapolis: Ukrainian Gift Shop, 2000.

Plokhy, Serhei. *The Gates of Europe: A History of Ukraine.* New York: Basic Books, 2021.

Subtelny, Orest. *Ukraine: A History,* 4th ed. Toronto: University of Toronto Press, 2009.

Vincent, Lynn, and Sara Vladic. *Indianapolis.* New York: Simon & Schuster, 2018.

MAGAZINES, NEWSPAPERS, JOURNALS, AND ARTICLES

*Berger, Meyer. "About New York: Ancient Art of Ukrainian Egg Jewelers, Still Popular, Goes on Exhibition Today." *New York Times,* November 7, 1955.

Ehrenhalt, Lizzie. "The storied connection between the Ukrainian community and Northeast Minneapolis." MinnPost.com, April 11, 2022.

Fornusek, Martin. "Ministry: Russia's war destroys or damages almost 2,000 cultural facilities." *Kyiv Independent,* May 2, 2024. kyivindependent.com/ministry-russias-war-destroys-or-damages-almost-2-000-cultural-sites.

*Jordan, Robert Paul. "Easter Greetings from the Ukrainians." *National Geographic,* April 1972.

Kaul, Greta. "How Northeast Minneapolis came to be a center of the Ukrainian-American community." MinnPost.com, March 2, 2022.

Pioneer Press. "In Roseville, keeping Ukrainian folk art of intricately painted eggs alive worldwide." April 23, 2011.

Tsioulcas, Anastasia. "These intricately decorated eggs are raising money and good wishes for Ukraine." NPR.org, April 12, 2022.

Ukrainian Gift Shop. "Our Family." ukrainiangiftshop.com.

Vargas, Theresa. "In Ukrainian eggs, people are finding a way to connect and help." *Washington Post,* March 30, 2022.

Waxman, Olivia B. "The History Behind the Ukrainian Tradition of Decorating Pysanky Easter Eggs." *Time,* April 14, 2022.

Zabelski, Katya. "How Ukrainian Folk Art Became a Tool of Resistance Against Russia." Hyperallergic.com, June 6, 2022.

Zielyk, Sofika. "A centuries-long tradition, a symbol of defiance." apofenie.com, May 19, 2023.

PERSONAL INTERVIEWS

Elko Perchyshyn, Jr., Marie's grandson, son of Luba Perchyshyn, and current owner of the Ukrainian Gift Shop.

*Natalie Perchyshyn, Marie's granddaughter, daughter of Luba Perchyshyn, and author of many books on pysanky.

*Ann Kmit, Marie's granddaughter, daughter of Johanna Luciow, and author of the Ukrainian Gift Shop's first pysanky books.

Tony Luciow, Marie's grandson, and son of Johanna Luciow.

Maria Matlashewski, daughter of Ukrainian refugee George Pasichnyk, whose family Marie and Tony sponsored to start new lives in Minneapolis.

Sofika Zielyk, ethnographer, pysanka artist, and museum collection curator.

VIDEO

Watch Marie Procai's daughter, Luba Perchyshyn, create a pysanka: forbes.com/sites/katyasoldak/2012/04/06/a-ukrainian-easter-egg-from-the-midwest/?sh=3e05d9a82110.

PICTURE CREDITS

Rich Wallace: 40. Hennepin County Library: 40, 41. US Navy: 42. Jim Sugar, Getty Images: 43. Ukrainian Gift Shop, Minneapolis Minnesota: 44 (top left and right, bottom right); Photo by Michael Liebig: 44 (bottom left).

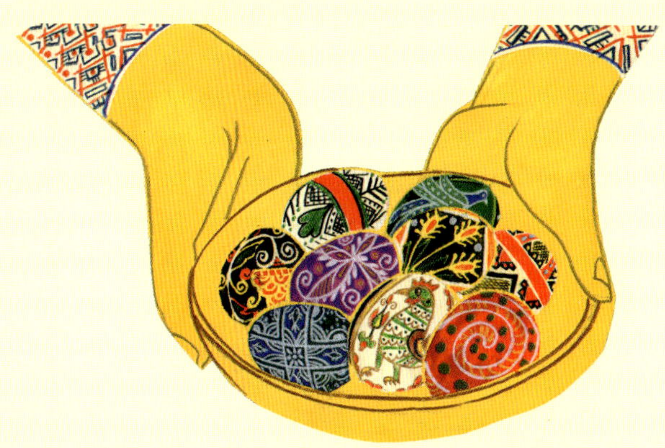

ACKNOWLEDGMENTS

I am grateful to Marie's family—Elko, Natalie, Ann, and Tony—for answering my many questions and confirming information about their grandmother. Thank you to ethnographer and pysanka artist Sofika Zielyk for reviewing the manuscript for cultural accuracy; Sue Godfrey of the Minnesota Discovery Center/Iron Range Research Center for helping me uncover more documents on Marie; the Arolsen Archives International Center on Nazi Persecution for access to the displaced persons records of so many Ukrainians whom Marie sponsored; and Maria Matlashewski for her oral history of her father's family, who were sponsored by Marie and Tony Procai.

A portion of my author proceeds will be donated to nonprofits preserving Ukrainian cultural identity through the art of pysanky and to nonprofits supporting Ukrainian refugees, including the Ukrainian National Women's League of America (UNWLA) and the Ukrainian Institute of America.

To my grandmother, Baba Neilipovitz, who, after spending all day working in the onion fields, created beauty at night embroidering ritual cloths with dazzling designs from her Ukrainian village, and who gifted us pysanky every Easter, written with love. —*SNW*

To the artists who create meaning and beauty in perilous times —*ET*

Calkins Creek
An imprint of Astra Books for Young Readers,
a division of Astra Publishing House
astrapublishinghouse.com
Printed in China

ISBN: 978-1-6626-8069-4 (hc)
ISBN: 978-1-6626-8070-0 (eBook)
Library of Congress Control Number: 2025935723

First edition

10 9 8 7 6 5 4 3 2 1

Design by Barbara Grzeslo and Melia Parsloe
The text is set in Kabel LT Std book.
The illustrations are done in gouache, resist, and colored pencil.